Mommy, please spend time with me!

Amelia's Adventures

By Amelia Di Blasio & Marge Di Blasio

Copyright © 2021 @ CreativeIBY

All rights reserved. No part of this publication may be reproduced, distributed or transmitted in any form or by any means, including photocopying, recording, or other electronic or mechanical methods, without the prior written permission of the publisher, except in the case of brief quotations embodied in critical reviews and certain other non-commercial uses permitted by copyright law.

Illustrated By Ishara Jayasinghe | Formatted By CreativeIBY
ISBN: 97817777509-2-3 (Paperback)
www.margediblasio.com/books

For Arwen, Amelia and all the other explorers,
never lose your curiosity.
For everything, there is a season.

The day that Amelia's didn't have school, she jumped out of her bed and looked forward to play.

"No school today!" yelled Amelia. I can do anything I want. Time to work on my projects!"

First, she put on her crown and dressed up like a princess. Then she played with her dolls. She danced around and read books about ponies.

Before Mommy could even respond to Amelia, the phone rang again. Mommy put Amelia down and hurried to answer the call.

Amelia couldn't wait for so long, so she walked to her room and picked up her best friend, Fuzzalina Teddy.

"Just a moment, just a moment!" cried Amelia. "Fuzzalina, I don't understand why Mommy needs to work!"

"Ouch, that was loud Amelia!" said Fuzzalina.

"I read all my books, played and did some colouring. Now I want Mommy but she is always working," said Amelia.

"Right! Someone is so upset," said Fuzzalina.
"Look around you Amelia."

"The clothes you wear, the toys you play with, the food you eat, the house you live, where do you think Mommy get all these?" asked Fuzzalina.

Amelia looked puzzled, so Fuzzalina continued. "She wanted to be with you, but she had to do what's best for you."

Amelia remembered that when Mommy took that job, she cried.

"She couldn't imagine you growing up without a nice place to stay, clothes to wear and food to eat. She realized, to give you the best life, she needed to provide for you," explained Fuzzalina.

Amelia finally realized what her Mommy does is also for her own good.

"Oh, I get it now," said Amelia. "Mommy works to give me a better life."

"Why don't you give her some time? Tell her what you feel," said Fuzzalina.

Amelia pondered on what Fuzzalina said. Then Mommy suddenly came back into her room.

"I'm sorry Honey. I had to take that call," said Mommy.

"Mommy, I know you have to work for us. I just wanted to have some time with you," Amelia explained.

Mommy realized that Amelia was needing her so much. She knew she could finish her work later on.

"How about I take a break now and let's spend time together?" asked Mommy.

"How about your work?" asked Amelia.

"I will catch up on it later when you're sleeping," said Mommy. "My work can wait; my little girl needs me more this time."

Amelia gave Mommy a big hug.

"Hurray! I'm going to spend time with Mommy!" said Amelia.

Amelia took her Mommy's hand and walked out the front door.

"Let's keep going Mommy," said Amelia.

They walked and walked and finally came to the park. They played on the swings.

They swooshed down the slide and went for a bike ride.

"Sometimes I have to do something else, but it doesn't mean I forgot you," Mommy said as they reached Amelia's room.
"Really Mommy?" asked Amelia.

"It might feel long for you to wait to see me once in a while, that's why I appreciate you being patient with me too. I know it's a lot for you," explained Mommy.

"Thank you for just being with me!" exclaimed Amelia. "You're the best Mommy ever!"

"I love you!" said Mommy.

They agreed to spend every weekend doing something fun together. Amelia realized that even though her Mommy has to do other things apart from her, she is never forgotten and her Mommy will always come back.

 Spot which two pictures of Amelia are exactly the same.

A.

B.

C.

D.

Answer: A and D

How about you my friend?
Did you spend some time with the people you care for?

Remember, Quality time being together is not measured by hours but how much undivided attention you give to each other.

Spending quality time with the people that matter to you is a decision only you can make.

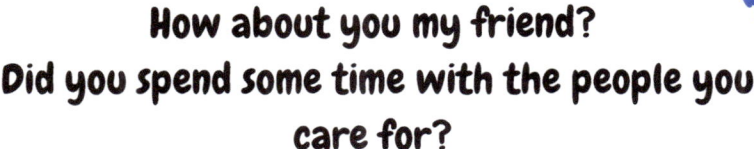

"Direct your children onto the right path, and when they are older, they will not leave it." Proverbs 22:6
"There is a time for everything..." - Ecclesiastes 3

One More Thing...

Thanks again for reading our book.
We would love to hear what you think.

Could you please take a moment to review?

Your feedback can help others to learn more about our book. It will also help us understand how we can do better and come up with more creative ideas to share with you and others.

Many thanks,
Amelia and Mommy

Other Recommended Books

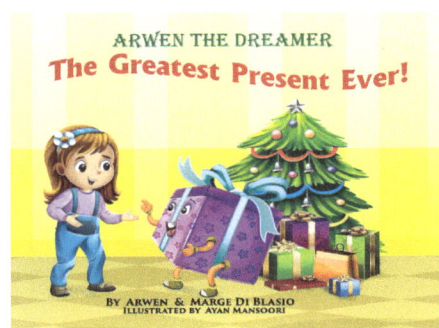 

About the Authors

AMELIA DI BLASIO is a young creator who loves to be around people and explore.
She enjoys dancing, reading, painting, swimming and most of all, to have fun.
Inspired by the books her family published, she wrote this book and collaborated with her mom when she was four years old.

MARGE CASTILLON DI BLASIO an author, coach, wife, mother, daughter, sister, friend, and a lifelong learner. While working as an IT Professional and raising her two lovely daughters, she got her real estate license and John Maxwell Team coaching certification. She publishes multiple books every year to encourage others who are going through dark times and to promote creativity.
She created this book to cultivate creativity together with her daughter, Amelia.
Learn more at www.margediblasio.com/books.

www.ingramcontent.com/pod-product-compliance
Lightning Source LLC
Chambersburg PA
CBHW042255100526
44589CB00002B/29